Contents

Words in bold, **like this**, are explained in the Glossary.

Why do animals have noses?

People and many animals have a nose. You use your nose for your **sense** of smell. You use your nose to **breathe**, too. People and animals need to breathe air to stay alive.

Animals' noses are different shapes and sizes. Some are large and some are small. Some can be difficult to see, but some are easy to spot. Mandrills like this one have a very colourful nose.

Nostrils

Many noses have two **nostrils**. These are passageways that begin as holes. When a moose **breathes**, air passes in and out of its nostrils. As the air comes into the moose's nostrils, it brings smells in too.

Ducks and other birds have nostrils, too.
Look for two small holes on top of the beak.
Ducks breathe through their nostrils when
they are not swimming underwater.

Protected noses

Many **nostrils** have hairs inside to keep out dirt when an animal **breathes** in. Hairs in the aardvark's nostrils keep soil out as it digs up **insects** to eat.

Manatees live in water but come to the
surface to breathe. They take in air through
their nostrils. When they dive, their nostrils
close to stop water getting in.

Sensitive noses

Many **mammals** have sensitive noses that can pick up all kinds of **scents**. Their **sense** of smell often helps them to find food. A polar bear can even smell a seal hiding under the ice.

Dogs have a very good sense of smell, too.
People train dogs to seek out one scent.
This dog is looking for the scent of a
missing person in the snow.

Pointed noses

The tiny elephant shrew uses its long, pointed nose to sniff out food. It likes to eat beetles, spiders and small animals. It pushes its nose in amongst dead leaves and rotting wood to find them.

The giant anteater has a very long, pointed nose. Its good **sense** of smell helps it to find the **insects** it eats. It pushes its nose into **termite** nests, so that it can lick up the termites inside.

Noses with flat ends

Flat-ended noses are useful for sniffing out food on the ground. Wild boars like these have a long nose with a flat end. They sniff the forest floor for acorns and roots. Then they dig them up with their nose and **tusks**.

People sometimes use pigs to help them find truffles. The pigs sniff the ground with their flat-ended noses to find the truffles. Truffles are a **fungus** that people like to eat.

Trunks

An elephant's trunk is made up of its nose and top lip. An elephant **breathes** through it. The long trunk can pull down tall branches of tasty leaves. The tip of the trunk can pick up small grains of rice.

A tapir has a strong trunk, but it is much
smaller than an elephant's. It uses its trunk
to sniff out and tear off tasty leaves to eat.

Noses on top

A hippopotamus likes to stay out of the hot sun by bathing. Its **nostrils** face upwards and stick out above the surface of the water. This allows it to **breathe** while it stays cool.

Crocodiles live in rivers and lakes. They often hide in the water, to catch their **prey**. All you can see are their nostrils, ears and eyes. Their nostrils stick out of the water so that they can breathe.

Blowholes

A whale's **nostrils** are called blowholes. They are on top of its head. Some whales have one blowhole, others have two. They use their blowholes to **breathe**.

Whales swim to the surface of the sea to
breathe in air. When the whale breathes
out, water lying on its head shoots up into
the air.

Noses underwater

Salmon are fish that swim long distances. Some return from the sea to the same river where they were born. They find the right river by smelling the water as it passes through their **nostrils**.

Eels use their nostrils to find their way, too. Some eels live in rivers and then swim to a special part of the sea to lay eggs. They use their **sense** of smell to get there.

Noses in the dark

A star mole hunts for food in the bottom of ponds. It uses the ring of pink feelers on its nose to feel its way around in the dark.

Badgers are **nocturnal**. At night, as it is dark, they sniff the forest floor to find food. Their sensitive noses pick up the **scents** of berries, worms, mice and **insects**.

Noisy noses

Noses sometimes help to make sounds. Some bats make sounds through their noses and then listen to the **echoes**. This helps them to find their way as they fly through the night sky.

A **male** elephant seal has an enormous
nose which hangs over its mouth. Its nose
makes the sound of its roar louder. Animals
several kilometres away can hear it.

How does it smell?

Moths have **antennae** instead of a nose to pick up smells. The feathery antennae of this **male** emperor moth picks up the **scent** of a **female** moth that is over a kilometre away.

A snake does not use its **nostrils** to smell. Instead, it flicks out its forked tongue to taste the air. It can pick up the scent of its **prey** with its tongue.

Fact file

- Fish don't have noses, but they do have **nostrils**. They use their nostrils to smell.

- Birds don't have noses, but they do have nostrils. They use their nostrils to **breathe**, and for the **sense** of smell.

- Some animal noses are called snouts. We talk about a snake having a snout, rather than a nose.

This seal can close its nostrils when it is underwater.

Glossary

antennae   feelers on top of an insect's head

breathe   take air in and out of the body

echoes   when sounds, such as a shout, come back through the air

female   a female parent is a mother

fungus   plant-like growth, such as a mushroom

insect   small animal with three main parts to its body, and six legs

male   a male parent is a father

mammals   animals that feed their babies with the mother's milk. People are mammals.

nocturnal   awake and active at night, rather than during the day

nostrils   passageways in the nose, through which animals may breathe or smell

prey   animals that are hunted for food

scent   a special kind of smell

sense   a way of being aware of the world (sight, hearing, smell, touch and taste are senses)

termite   an insect that lives in very large groups

tusk   very large tooth that sticks out of an animal's mouth

Index